CITYSCAPE OF TRIUMPH:

"MIKE'S JOURNEY THROUGH ENTREPRENEURIAL RESILIENCE"

By

DR FAITH STONES

Copyright © 2023

Table Of Contents

□ **Introducing Cityscape of Triumph: "Mike's Journey Through Entrepreneurial Resilience"**□

Embark on a riveting journey through the bustling metropolis of success, where towering skyscrapers mirror the heights of triumph, and city lights illuminate the path of resilience. In this compelling novel, "Cityscape of Triumph," we follow the relentless pursuit of dreams by Mike, a resilient entrepreneur whose world crumbles only to be rebuilt with unwavering determination.

□□ **Explore the Urban Saga of Resilience**
□□

Step into the heart of Mike's entrepreneurial odyssey as he navigates the labyrinth of success and failure. From the zenith of prosperity to the depths of bankruptcy, each chapter unfolds like a cityscape, revealing the vibrant tapestry of Mike's journey.

☐ **Discover New Horizons Amidst Setbacks** ☐

Amidst initial struggles, emotional turmoil, and the shadows of doubt, Mike discovers a new passion, setting the stage for a narrative that blends the personal and professional. Skepticism, challenges, and strategic leaps weave a plot that mirrors the complexities of real-world entrepreneurship.

☐ **Witness Triumphs and Setbacks in the City Lights** ☐

As Mike faces skepticism, takes daring leaps, and confronts the biggest challenges of his career, the city lights become a backdrop to his victories and setbacks. The narrative is a symphony of small wins, transformative alliances, and the grit needed to thrive in a dynamic urban landscape.

☐ **Climax in the Heart of the City** ☐

The climactic chapters reveal a resolute Mike confronting fears, adapting to changing circumstances, and ultimately triumphing against all odds. The city transforms from a witness to an active participant in the triumph of resilience, marking the climax of an extraordinary journey.

 □ **Celebrate Major Successes in the City of Dreams** □

In the finale, "Cityscape of Triumph" celebrates major successes, portraying a narrative where not only does Mike's business survive, but it thrives. The city becomes a canvas of jubilation, mirroring the collective joy of triumph that reverberates within the entrepreneurial journey.

 □ **Join Mike's Journey, Where Resilience Meets Triumph** □

"Cityscape of Triumph" is not just a novel; it's an immersive exploration of the human spirit, entrepreneurial resilience, and the triumphs that await those who dare to dream. Get ready to navigate the city lights, witness the skyline of success, and be inspired by a story that resonates with the beating heart of every entrepreneur.

Dive into "Cityscape of Triumph" and let the urban symphony of resilience captivate your imagination. 🏙️🌃

Chapter 1:

A HEIGHTS TO FALL FROM

The sun dipped below the horizon, casting long shadows across the city skyline. Amidst the hustle and bustle of downtown, one figure stood tall—Mike Anderson, a titan of the business world. His empire, Anderson Innovations, was etched into the urban landscape like a beacon of success.

Mike, with his sharp mind and decisive demeanor, had carved a niche for himself in the tech industry. His company's innovations were the talk of boardrooms, and his name echoed in admiration across business circles. Tall and lean, with salt-and-pepper hair that spoke of experience rather than age, Mike was the embodiment of the American Dream.

As the CEO of Anderson Innovations, Mike's office on the top floor of a gleaming skyscraper afforded him a panoramic view of the city below. The expansive glass windows framed a world he had conquered through sheer determination and foresight. Awards adorned his office walls, a testament to his business acumen and the countless hours he had poured into building his empire.

The story of Mike's rise to success wasn't just a narrative of profits and losses; it was a saga of grit, risk-taking, and unwavering commitment. Born into a modest family, Mike had defied the odds, fueled by an unrelenting ambition to turn dreams into reality. He had started Anderson Innovations from scratch, fueled by an insatiable curiosity and a belief that technology could shape the future.

As the chapter unfolds, the reader witnesses Mike navigating through the intricate dance of corporate meetings, sealing deals with a firm handshake and a confident smile. His charisma was magnetic, drawing people into his vision for a future where technology seamlessly integrated with daily life.

The success, however, came at a cost. The long hours, the missed family dinners, the sacrifices—each brick in the towering edifice of Anderson Innovations had a story to tell. Mike's personal life bore the scars of his relentless pursuit of success. Relationships strained by the weight of his responsibilities, and the echoes of laughter from family gatherings became distant memories.

Despite the challenges, Mike's empire flourished. Anderson Innovations became synonymous with innovation itself, and Mike basked in the glory of a hard-fought victory. His face graced magazine covers, and he became a sought-after speaker at conferences, sharing the secrets of his triumph with aspiring entrepreneurs.

Yet, as the city lights glittered below his penthouse, a shadow loomed—a harbinger of the storm that would shake the foundations of Mike's world. Little did he know that the very empire he had built with sweat and determination would face a reckoning, propelling him into a journey of self-discovery and resilience.

The chapter concludes with Mike, standing by the window, contemplating the cityscape. The silhouette of success outlined by the setting sun was about to be engulfed by the darkness of unforeseen challenges, setting the stage for a narrative that would explore the depths of Mike's character and the true measure of success.

Chapter 2:

THE TUMULTUOUS FALL

The morning sun, once a herald of triumph, now cast long, ominous shadows in Mike's office. The air hung heavy with tension as news of a crisis reached the upper echelons of Anderson Innovations. Mike, typically the orchestrator of order, found himself at the epicenter of chaos.

The crisis had arrived like a stealthy thief in the night, gradually unraveling the very fabric of his meticulously built empire. It began with a series of unforeseen market shifts, a sudden downturn that sent shockwaves through the financial world. Whispers of economic instability morphed into a deafening roar, and the once-stable ground beneath Anderson Innovations quivered.

As the chapter opens, Mike navigates through a maze of emergency meetings and crisis management. His usually unshakeable composure strained, he grapples with the harsh reality that his empire, once considered impervious, is now vulnerable. The news headlines scream of impending doom, and the stock prices of Anderson Innovations plummet like a falling star.

In the midst of the chaos, Mike's leadership is put to the ultimate test. Layoffs become inevitable, and the once-thriving offices echo with the footsteps of departing employees. The faces of loyal colleagues, who had stood by him through the glory days, now reflect uncertainty and fear.

The walls of his corner office, adorned with accolades and symbols of success, seem to close in. The weight of responsibility bears down on Mike, as he grapples with the realization that he might not be able to salvage the ship he worked so hard to build. The sense of impending failure is a bitter pill, and the taste is all the more bitter when accompanied by the bitter truths of corporate dynamics.

Amidst the financial turmoil, personal sacrifices pile up. The late nights at the office stretch into early mornings, and the distance between Mike and his family grows. The once-celebrated entrepreneur becomes a prisoner of his own circumstances, a captive of a situation he couldn't have predicted.

The chapter delves into the human side of the crisis. Mike, who once stood tall among his employees, now walks through the deserted hallways, contemplating the personal toll of corporate upheaval. Faces of colleagues and friends flash before his eyes, each departure a reminder of the interconnected lives that his decisions impact.

As the crisis deepens, the boardroom transforms into a battlefield of strategic maneuvers and desperate attempts to stay afloat. Mike, a captain navigating treacherous waters, grapples with tough decisions. The weight of each choice is palpable, as he considers the livelihoods of loyal employees versus the survival of the company.

The chapter concludes with Mike, alone in his dimly lit office, staring at the city skyline that once symbolized his success. The silent witness to his triumphs now bore witness to the unraveling of his dreams. The fall from grace was complete, leaving Mike at the precipice of a journey he never anticipated—one that would test not only his business acumen but the very core of his resilience and determination.

Chapter 3:

SHATTERED FOUNDATIONS

The aftermath of the crisis envelops Mike's life in a haze of uncertainty and shattered expectations. The once-bustling offices of Anderson Innovations are now haunted by echoes of former vitality. As Chapter 3 unfolds, the readers witness Mike navigating the wreckage of his once-thriving empire, grappling with both external challenges and the internal storm of emotions.

The chapter opens with Mike surveying the deserted offices. Empty desks and dimmed screens paint a stark picture of the fallout. The weight of the past success now bears down on his shoulders, and the once-imposing office feels like a cavernous echo chamber of regrets. Mike, who once strode confidently through these halls, now moves with a heavy gait, burdened by the weight of responsibility and the ghosts of decisions past.

The financial strain becomes tangible as Mike confronts the reality of downsizing. Colleagues-turned-friends, their faces etched with disappointment, file out of the building with cardboard boxes in hand. Each departure is a testament to the human cost of corporate failure, and Mike is forced to confront the personal toll of his decisions. The emotional toll of letting loyal employees go weighs heavily on his conscience.

As Mike grapples with the logistics of winding down projects and closing departments, the emotional toll spills over into his personal life. The once-happy home becomes a battleground of tension and unspoken fears. Mike's spouse, who had stood by him through the glory days, now looks at him with a mix of concern and disappointment. The strains on family life intensify as financial pressures mount.

The chapter explores Mike's internal struggle, his mind a tempest of self-doubt and regrets. Sleepless nights are spent staring at the ceiling, haunted by the faces of former employees and the implications of the choices he made. The dreams that once fueled his ambition now morph into nightmares, each one a distorted reflection of the success he once took for granted.

As Mike contemplates the wreckage of his business, he is faced with the daunting task of reinventing himself. The business world that once bowed to his vision now casts a skeptical gaze. Networking events become a battlefield of awkward conversations and sidelong glances. Mike, who was once the epitome of confidence, now wears the cloak of uncertainty.

In a desperate attempt to find solace, Mike seeks the advice of mentors and peers. The once-expansive network that admired his success now offers sympathetic nods and hesitant words of encouragement. Mike, who had been the one doling out advice, now finds himself on the receiving end, a humbling experience that further chips away at his pride.

The chapter reaches its emotional climax as Mike, in a moment of vulnerability, confronts the mirror. The reflection staring back is a stark contrast to the confident executive he once knew. The lines on his face tell the story of sleepless nights, and the eyes reflect the weight of the world on his shoulders. The emotional turmoil within is a tempest that threatens to consume him.

The closing scenes of the chapter set the stage for Mike's journey of redemption. As he confronts the wreckage of his past success and the emotional toll of his decisions, a spark of resilience glimmers in his eyes. The journey ahead is uncertain, but Mike, battered and bruised, stands ready to face the storm, determined to rebuild not just his business but the shattered fragments of his identity.

Chapter 4:

REFLECTIONS IN THE AFTERMATH

With the debris of Anderson Innovations scattered behind him, Mike finds himself at a crossroads. Chapter 4 opens with him retreating from the chaos, seeking solitude in the places that once inspired his visions of success. The city, once a canvas for his dreams, now mirrors his inner turmoil.

As Mike reflects on his life, the chapter delves into the recesses of his past, unraveling the threads that wove the fabric of his ambition. Flashbacks transport the reader to a time when a young Mike, fueled by determination, set out to defy the limitations of his modest beginnings. His dreams were skyscrapers, reaching for the heights of success.

The narrative unfolds as Mike revisits pivotal moments—late nights at the kitchen table sketching business plans, the adrenaline-fueled pitches to skeptical investors, and the joyous celebrations of each milestone conquered. Success was a ladder he climbed, rung by rung, and each step was a testament to his unyielding will.

Yet, as the chapter progresses, the narrative takes a poignant turn. The same dreams that once propelled him forward become a haunting reminder of what was lost. The city, bathed in the golden glow of sunset, now casts long shadows over his aspirations. The very buildings that bore witness to his triumphs stand as silent spectators to his fall.

Amidst the wreckage of his goals, Mike confronts the question of identity. The relentless pursuit of success had molded him into the formidable entrepreneur the world knew, but now, stripped of the titles and accolades, he faces the challenge of rediscovering who he truly is. The process is a journey inward, an excavation of layers built by years of ambition and accomplishment.

The chapter navigates Mike's introspection, his thoughts a whirlwind of self-discovery and introspective musings. What were once clear-cut goals now blur into existential questions. The definition of success, once measured in profit margins and market shares, undergoes a metamorphosis. The metrics of success, it seems, were not immune to the shifting tides that rocked his business.

As he contemplates his past, Mike is confronted by the ghosts of choices made. The sacrifices that seemed noble in the pursuit of success now cast a somber shadow. The missed family dinners, the strained relationships, and the toll on his own well-being—all laid bare in the harsh light of retrospection. The chapter peels back the layers of the successful facade, exposing the vulnerabilities beneath.

In a poignant moment, Mike revisits a letter he wrote to his younger self—a manifesto of dreams and ambitions. The words, once a source of inspiration, now read like an ancient script from another lifetime. The dissonance between the aspirations of the past and the reality of the present weighs heavily on his shoulders.

Yet, in the midst of the reflection, a glimmer of resilience emerges. The city, once a symbol of unattainable heights, becomes a canvas for reinvention. The skyline, though cast in shadows, hints at the possibility of a new dawn. The chapter concludes with Mike, standing on the precipice of self-discovery, ready to redefine his goals not in the pursuit of external validation but in alignment with the values that survived the storm—the true measure of success yet to be unveiled.

Chapter 5:

EMBERS OF PASSION

In the wake of shattered dreams, Mike finds solace in the unlikeliest of places. The chapter opens with him navigating the city streets, each step a deliberate act of rediscovery. The urban landscape, once a battleground of corporate conquests, becomes a playground for the exploration of newfound passions and opportunities.

As Mike immerses himself in the world outside boardrooms and executive offices, the narrative unfolds to reveal chance encounters that spark the embers of a dormant passion. The city, with its vibrant communities and diverse subcultures, becomes a tapestry of inspiration waiting to be woven into a new narrative.

The chapter introduces the reader to Mike's unexpected forays into uncharted territory. A chance visit to a local art gallery exposes him to the world of creativity and expression. The colors on canvas and the stories behind each piece resonate with a part of him that lay dormant beneath the corporate armor. Mike, who once calculated success in profit margins, now finds himself drawn to the intangible beauty of artistic creation.

The city's eclectic neighborhoods become classrooms, and Mike, the eternal learner, immerses himself in diverse skill sets. From cooking classes in a bohemian district to joining a community gardening project, each experience becomes a brushstroke in the canvas of his reinvention. The newfound passion for these pursuits sparks a vitality long absent from his life.

In the midst of this exploration, Mike stumbles upon a group of entrepreneurs crafting a different narrative. A tech incubator in a repurposed warehouse becomes the breeding ground for innovative ideas and collaborative spirit. The entrepreneurs, unburdened by the weight of traditional success metrics, are driven by a shared passion for impact and innovation.

As the chapter unfolds, Mike becomes entwined with this community of forward-thinkers. The air in the incubator buzzes with the energy of creativity, and Mike, once confined by the rigidity of corporate structures, finds himself liberated by the spirit of collaboration. The shared pursuit of meaningful projects becomes a balm for the wounds of past failures.

Amidst this new venture, the reader witnesses the rekindling of Mike's entrepreneurial spirit. The projects, born not out of profit motives but a genuine desire to make a positive impact, breathe life into his vision. The narrative explores the joy of creation, the satisfaction of solving real-world problems, and the camaraderie forged in the crucible of shared passion.

The chapter highlights pivotal moments where Mike's perspective shifts. The metrics of success transform from financial gains to the tangible impact on communities. The passion for innovation, once overshadowed by the pursuit of wealth, becomes the driving force behind each endeavor. Mike, once a captain navigating the turbulent seas of corporate competition, now finds himself part of a collective journey toward a shared vision.

The city, once a backdrop for cutthroat business dealings, now becomes a stage for Mike's reinvention. From the murals adorning forgotten alleyways to the vibrant street performances, each aspect of urban life becomes a source of inspiration. The chapter weaves together these threads of newfound passion, painting a picture of a man shedding the armor of past success to embrace the vulnerability of authentic self-discovery.

As the chapter concludes, Mike stands at the intersection of past and present, the embers of passion now a flickering flame. The city, once a labyrinth of challenges, is now a playground for possibilities. The entrepreneurial journey takes on a new meaning—one defined not only by financial gains but by the fulfillment found in pursuing a purpose-driven path. The reader is left with a sense of anticipation, eager to witness the unfolding chapters of Mike's reinvention, fueled by the flames of newfound passion and opportunity.

Chapter 6:

NAVIGATING DOUBTFUL TIDES

In the wake of Mike's newfound passion and ventures, the canvas of his life is painted with vibrant strokes of change. However, as the chapter unfolds, the narrative takes a poignant turn as Mike confronts a new challenge—skepticism from those closest to him. The support network that once celebrated his triumphs now casts doubtful glances, creating turbulent waters in the sea of his reinvention.

The chapter opens with Mike excitedly sharing his vision with friends and family. The once-confident entrepreneur is now a beacon of enthusiasm, eager to convey the transformative power of his new pursuits. However, the

response he receives is far from the validation he
anticipates.

Friends, accustomed to the image of the
successful corporate magnate, raise eyebrows at
the unconventional path he is treading. Family
members, who once reveled in the prestige of
Anderson Innovations, express concern over the
perceived instability of his new ventures. The
skepticism, like a chill wind, cuts through the
warmth of Mike's excitement.

The narrative explores the dynamics of these
interactions, delving into the dialogues and
unspoken tensions that arise. Mike's attempts to
articulate the shift in his priorities and the
fulfillment he finds in his current endeavors are
met with furrowed brows and hesitant nods. The
dissonance between the expectations of others
and the authenticity of his journey becomes a
central theme.

As the chapter progresses, Mike grapples with
the weight of external expectations. The

questions from well-meaning friends echo in his mind—Why leave the safety of a well-established career? What about the financial stability of your family? The doubts planted by those he values most become seeds of uncertainty, threatening to overshadow the flourishing garden of his newfound passion.

The narrative shifts to intimate scenes where Mike engages in heartfelt conversations with loved ones. The dinner table, once a hub of celebration, becomes a battleground of conflicting visions. Spousal conversations are laced with unspoken fears, and the emotional toll of navigating skepticism from those closest to him becomes palpable.

The chapter doesn't shy away from the vulnerability Mike experiences. The inner conflict between the desire for approval and the need for authenticity becomes a crucible of self-discovery. The once-resilient entrepreneur now grapples with doubts that cut deeper than any external critique. The reader is drawn into the internal monologue, witnessing the battle between staying true to oneself and conforming to societal expectations.

Amidst the skepticism, the narrative introduces pivotal moments where Mike draws strength from within. Encounters with like-minded individuals who share his passion become pillars of support. Mentors from the entrepreneurial community, who have trodden similar paths, offer guidance and assurance. These scenes become beacons of hope, illuminating the path forward amid the fog of doubt.

The chapter also touches upon the resilience required to weather these skeptical tides. Mike, though momentarily shaken, begins to develop a thicker skin. The once-glistening armor of corporate success now transforms into a shield, protecting the ember of his passion from the gusts of doubt. The narrative underscores the transformative power of adversity, sculpting Mike into a more resilient version of himself.

As the chapter draws to a close, the reader is left with a sense of anticipation. The skepticism from friends and family remains a lingering cloud, but the ember of Mike's passion continues to burn. The cityscape, now a backdrop to the internal and external storms, sets the stage for the unfolding chapters of Mike's journey. The reader is left wondering whether the flames of authenticity will eventually dispel the clouds of doubt or if they will be extinguished by the weight of skepticism.

Chapter 7:

A LEAP OF FAITH

In the crucible of skepticism and self-discovery, Mike stands at a precipice, facing the daunting expansc of thc unknown. Chapter 7 opens with a sense of anticipation as he contemplates the decision to take a leap into a new venture. The city, a backdrop to his journey, holds its breath, mirroring the tension that permeates the air.

The narrative unfolds with Mike wrestling with the dual forces of doubt and determination. The doubts sown by friends and family echo in his mind, but the ember of passion within refuses to be extinguished. Scenes transition between intimate moments of reflection and the vibrant energy of the city, creating a tapestry that captures the dichotomy of his internal struggle.

The chapter introduces a cast of supporting characters who become instrumental in Mike's decision-making process. Mentors from the entrepreneurial community provide guidance, sharing their own stories of risk and reward. Friends who initially expressed skepticism now offer cautious encouragement, their doubts tempered by a glimmer of curiosity about the uncharted territory Mike is venturing into.

As Mike explores potential ventures, the narrative delves into the selection process. Scenes unfold in bustling co-working spaces, coffee shops buzzing with creative energy, and collaborative meetings with visionaries who share his passion. Each encounter becomes a stepping stone, narrowing down the possibilities and refining the vision that will define his leap into the unknown.

The city, depicted as both a backdrop and a character in itself, plays a crucial role in this decision-making process. Rooftop views provide moments of solitude for introspection, and the hum of city life serves as a soundtrack to the symphony of ideas germinating in Mike's mind. The urban landscape becomes a metaphor for the boundless opportunities awaiting him.

The narrative builds tension as Mike reaches the moment of decision. The reader is led through the emotional turmoil of sleepless nights and restless contemplation. The turning point is marked by a scene where Mike, fueled by a newfound sense of purpose, faces the mirror with a determined gaze. The reflection staring back is not just a man, but an entrepreneur poised to redefine success on his own terms.

The chapter climaxes with the dramatic leap—a decision to pursue a venture aligned with his passion. The scene is set in a symbolic location, perhaps a rooftop overlooking the cityscape, where Mike, surrounded by the glow of city lights, embraces the uncertainty that lies ahead. The city, an unwavering witness to his journey, stands as a silent ally in this pivotal moment.

As Mike takes the plunge, the narrative captures the mix of exhilaration and fear that accompanies such a leap. The scenes transition between the rush of adrenaline as he finalizes the decision and the quieter moments of introspection, where the weight of the unknown bears down on him. The emotional rollercoaster becomes palpable, drawing the reader into the complex emotions of embracing change.

The chapter concludes with a sense of both closure and open-ended possibility. The decision to leap into a new venture is made, but the true impact remains to be seen. The city, now a landscape transformed by the night, is a canvas awaiting the strokes of Mike's reinvention. The reader is left on the edge of anticipation, eager to witness the unfolding chapters that will define the trajectory of Mike's entrepreneurial journey.

Chapter 8:

NAVIGATING THE RAPIDS

The dawn of Mike's new venture is greeted by the harsh light of reality. Chapter 8 opens with him stepping into the uncharted waters of entrepreneurship, each stride echoing with the uncertainty of the path ahead. The city, now awake with the hustle of a new day, becomes the backdrop to the initial challenges that unfold in this chapter.

The narrative sets the tone with scenes of Mike establishing the foundations of his new endeavor. The juxtaposition of the vibrant co-working space against the blank canvas of a startup's early days creates a visual metaphor for the potential waiting to be unlocked. The chapter captures the energy of innovation as desks are arranged, ideas are exchanged, and the hum of creativity becomes the heartbeat of this embryonic venture.

However, as the chapter unfolds, the narrative confronts the inevitable challenges that accompany the birth of any venture. The initial excitement is met with the reality of resource constraints, technical hurdles, and the unpredictable currents of the market. Mike, once the captain of a well-established ship, finds himself navigating the rapids of uncertainty.

The reader is introduced to a cast of characters integral to this phase of the journey—passionate team members who share Mike's vision. The camaraderie and shared sense of purpose become beacons of hope as they collectively face the challenges that arise. Scenes transition between moments of collaboration and the quiet determination that defines their shared mission.

The city, depicted in this chapter as a living organism, becomes a playground for testing ideas. Scenes unfold in bustling cafes where brainstorming sessions transform into action plans. The pulse of the city, captured in the rhythm of footsteps on busy sidewalks and the murmur of conversations, becomes a steady beat guiding their progress.

The narrative explores the vulnerability inherent in these early stages. Mike, accustomed to the well-established routines of his past, grapples with the fluidity of startup life. Sleepless nights are spent troubleshooting technical glitches and refining the pitch for potential investors. The weight of responsibility bears down on him as he faces the challenge of balancing optimism with the pragmatic realities of the entrepreneurial journey.

The chapter introduces key milestones and setbacks, each shaping the trajectory of the new venture. The first pitch to investors is met with mixed responses, and the rejection letters become a testament to the resilience required in the face of adversity. The reader witnesses the emotional rollercoaster as Mike and his team celebrate small victories, such as securing the first client, while confronting the disappointments of setbacks.

Amidst the challenges, the narrative interweaves scenes of personal growth. Mike, stripped of the trappings of his past success, becomes a more adaptable and empathetic leader. The vulnerability of the startup environment fosters a culture of open communication and a willingness to learn from failures. The once rigid executive transforms into a captain who shares both the risks and rewards with his team.

As the chapter progresses, the reader is drawn into the dynamics of the startup ecosystem. Networking events become opportunities for strategic alliances, and chance encounters with industry influencers provide insights that shape their approach. The city, depicted in this phase as a labyrinth of connections, becomes a source of both challenges and possibilities.

The chapter reaches a climactic moment as Mike and his team confront a significant obstacle that threatens the viability of the venture. The scene is set against the backdrop of a pivotal meeting with potential investors. The tension is palpable as they navigate the delicate dance of presenting their vision while acknowledging the hurdles they face. The outcome becomes a turning point, determining whether the venture will weather the storm or succumb to the rapids.

As the chapter concludes, the reader is left with a sense of both accomplishment and anticipation. The initial challenges have forged a tighter bond among the team, and the cityscape, now illuminated by the glow of streetlights, stands witness to the resilience of this nascent endeavor. The reader is left on the edge of curiosity, eager to discover how Mike and his team will navigate the unpredictable currents that lie ahead in the entrepreneurial journey.

Chapter 9:

THE UNYIELDING RESOLVE

Amidst the trials and tribulations of the entrepreneurial journey, Mike's spirit refuses to be dampened. Chapter 9 opens with a renewed determination that echoes through the corridors of his fledgling venture. The city, both witness and accomplice, sets the stage for a chapter defined by resilience and unyielding resolve.

The narrative unfolds as Mike faces the aftermath of the pivotal investor meeting. The city skyline, bathed in the glow of dawn, becomes a symbol of hope as he reflects on the challenges overcome and those that still lie ahead. The chapter captures the essence of Mike's growth—the evolution from a captain navigating stormy waters to a leader undeterred by setbacks.

Scenes transition between moments of strategic planning within the vibrant co-working space and solitary walks along the city's riverbanks. The metropolis, painted with hues of dawn and dusk, becomes a metaphor for the ebb and flow of the entrepreneurial journey. The reader is drawn into Mike's introspection, witnessing the evolution of his determination against the backdrop of the urban landscape.

The narrative introduces pivotal moments where Mike's leadership style undergoes a transformation. Team meetings become forums for collaborative problem-solving, where every setback is viewed as an opportunity to learn and iterate. The once-stern countenance softens into a blend of resilience and empathy, fostering a culture that thrives on shared determination.

The challenges faced by the venture become stepping stones for personal and professional growth. The reader is led through scenes of Mike diving into the intricacies of product development, working side by side with the team to troubleshoot technical glitches, and immersing himself in the dynamic landscape of marketing strategies. The chapter unfolds as a testament to his hands-on approach and the willingness to adapt to the ever-changing landscape of startup life.

Amidst the hustle and bustle of daily operations, the chapter explores the relationships that become the scaffolding of Mike's determination. Scenes depict camaraderie within the team, where shared goals and shared challenges strengthen the bonds forged in the crucible of entrepreneurship. The reader witnesses the unwavering support of teammates who believe not just in the vision of the venture but in each other.

As the venture faces external pressures—market shifts, unexpected competition, and the ever-present specter of uncertainty—Mike's resolve is tested. The city, depicted as a dynamic entity mirroring the turbulence of the business world, becomes a stage for Mike's unyielding determination. Scenes unfold in coffee shops where late-night strategy sessions blur into early morning brainstorming, highlighting the relentless pursuit of success.

The chapter delves into moments where Mike draws inspiration from unexpected sources. Chance encounters with industry veterans become valuable lessons, and the city's events and meetups transform into arenas for networking and knowledge exchange. The reader is invited to witness the mosaic of influences that shape Mike's evolving approach, underscoring the importance of adaptability in the entrepreneurial landscape.

The narrative also explores the personal sacrifices woven into the fabric of determination. The strains on Mike's personal life persist, but the chapter reveals a nuanced portrayal of balance. Scenes unfold where he carves out moments for family, acknowledging the importance of maintaining connections beyond the confines of the startup world. The reader is drawn into the complexity of juggling passion and responsibility.

Amidst the crescendo of challenges and triumphs, the chapter builds to a poignant scene where Mike addresses the team. The vibrancy of the co-working space becomes a canvas for his words, and the passion in his voice resonates with each team member. The speech becomes a rallying cry, a manifestation of the unyielding resolve that defines their collective journey.

As the chapter concludes, the reader is left with a sense of both accomplishment and anticipation. The venture, though still navigating the unpredictable currents of the business world, is buoyed by a determination that refuses to be extinguished. The cityscape, now aglow with the lights of opportunity, stands witness to the tenacity of Mike's spirit. The reader is left on the cusp of curiosity, eager to discover how this unyielding resolve will shape the chapters that lie ahead in the ongoing narrative of entrepreneurship.

Chapter 10:

DANCE OF SMALL VICTORIES AND SETBACKS

The journey of Mike's venture unfolds in the delicate dance between small victories and setbacks. Chapter 10 opens with the cityscape painted in the hues of a sunset, mirroring the nuanced rhythm of the entrepreneurial narrative. The streets, alive with the ebb and flow of urban life, become the stage for a chapter defined by the subtle interplay of progress and challenges.

The narrative takes the reader through scenes of incremental successes—landing a key client, achieving a milestone in product development, and witnessing the positive impact of their venture on a small scale. Each small victory becomes a brushstroke on the canvas of their journey, painting a picture of progress against the backdrop of the city's ever-changing skyline.

Scenes unfold in the vibrant co-working space, where the hum of creative energy serves as the soundtrack to their daily efforts. The reader is immersed in moments of collaboration, where team members celebrate achievements and troubleshoot challenges with equal fervor. The camaraderie within the team becomes a cornerstone of resilience, transforming setbacks into opportunities for growth.

As the chapter progresses, the narrative explores the external forces that shape the trajectory of the venture. Market dynamics, customer feedback, and the unpredictable currents of the business world become formidable opponents. Scenes transition between the excitement of securing a new partnership and the introspection that follows a setback, highlighting the fragile equilibrium between progress and the ever-present specter of obstacles.

The city, depicted as a living entity, becomes a metaphor for the complexities of entrepreneurship. Scenes unfold in coffee shops where discussions on strategy blur into the background noise of city life. The skyline, visible through the office windows, becomes a silent witness to the highs and lows of the entrepreneurial journey. The reader is drawn into the pulse of the urban environment, where each victory reverberates and each setback echoes.

The narrative introduces key characters who play pivotal roles in this delicate dance. Mentors from the entrepreneurial community provide guidance during setbacks, offering wisdom gleaned from their own experiences. Clients, whose satisfaction becomes a measure of success, offer feedback that shapes the evolution of the venture. The city's events and networking opportunities become arenas for forging alliances and overcoming obstacles.

As the venture gains traction, the reader witnesses the evolution of Mike's leadership style. The once-stern executive becomes a beacon of positivity, acknowledging the value of each small victory and instilling a sense of resilience within the team. Scenes unfold where Mike, in the face of setbacks, delivers motivational talks that rekindle the flame of determination.

The chapter navigates through scenes of adaptability and innovation. The team, fueled by the spirit of entrepreneurship, pivots in response to feedback, iterates on product designs, and experiments with marketing strategies. The city, with its constant flux, becomes a muse for creative solutions, and the narrative underscores the importance of agility in the face of change.

Intertwined with the victories are scenes of setbacks that threaten to cast shadows on their journey. The loss of a key client, technical glitches, and the ever-present challenge of securing funding become formidable adversaries. The reader is led through the emotional rollercoaster that accompanies each setback, from the initial shock to the determination that follows.

Amidst the complexities, the chapter explores the personal toll of the entrepreneurial journey. The strains on personal relationships persist, but the narrative paints a nuanced picture of resilience on the home front. Scenes unfold where Mike, though faced with challenges, finds solace in the support of his family—a support system that becomes a pillar of strength during the inevitable lows.

As the chapter reaches its climax, the reader is presented with a pivotal moment—a scene where Mike addresses the team in the wake of a setback. The cityscape, illuminated by the glow of city lights, becomes a backdrop to his words of encouragement. The speech becomes a testament to the resilience forged in the crucible of small victories and setbacks, marking a turning point in the trajectory of their journey.

The chapter concludes with a sense of both reflection and anticipation. The city, depicted as a tapestry of lights, stands as a silent witness to the ongoing dance of entrepreneurship. The reader is left on the edge of curiosity, eager to discover how the delicate interplay of small victories and setbacks will shape the chapters that unfold in the evolving narrative of Mike's venture.

Chapter 11:

FORGING ALLIANCES AND PARTNERSHIPS

In the ever-evolving tapestry of Mike's entrepreneurial journey, Chapter 11 unfolds against a backdrop of strategic collaborations and the forging of key alliances. The city, depicted as a hub of opportunity, becomes the canvas for this chapter, where every street corner holds the potential for meaningful connections that could shape the trajectory of the venture.

The narrative opens with scenes of Mike navigating networking events, each handshake and exchange of business cards a potential bridge to new possibilities. The city's skyline, visible through the venue's expansive windows, becomes a metaphor for the expansive landscape of opportunities waiting to be explored. The chapter sets a tone of anticipation as Mike steps into a world of partnerships that could redefine the course of his venture.

As the chapter progresses, the narrative introduces key characters who become instrumental in this phase of the journey. Scenes unfold in dynamic co-working spaces where conversations with fellow entrepreneurs transform into collaborative ventures. Mentors, whose insights go beyond advice to tangible support, become pillars of strength. The city's vibrant ecosystem of innovation becomes a playground for strategic alliances.

The reader is drawn into the intricacies of partnership negotiations, where discussions range from shared visions to the nitty-gritty details of collaboration. Scenes transition between the high-energy buzz of partnership pitches and the quieter moments of contemplation as Mike weighs the potential benefits and risks of each alliance. The city, depicted as a bustling marketplace of ideas, becomes a testament to the transformative power of collaboration.

The narrative unfolds as Mike navigates the dance of diplomacy, understanding that successful partnerships are not just about aligning interests but also about the synergy of values and goals. Scenes depict him refining pitches, tailoring them to suit the unique strengths of potential collaborators. The city, a mosaic of diverse industries and perspectives, becomes a source of inspiration for innovative approaches to partnership building.

The chapter highlights moments where the venture's value proposition resonates with potential partners. The first inkling of shared enthusiasm becomes a turning point, and scenes unfold where handshakes symbolize not just agreements but the birth of collaborative ventures. The reader is led through the emotional highs of these victories, each partnership a testament to the potential of collective innovation.

Amidst the successes, the narrative explores setbacks and negotiations that don't materialize into partnerships. Scenes unfold in coffee shops and office spaces where Mike, undeterred by rejection, refines his approach and learns from each experience. The city, with its ever-changing dynamics, becomes a reminder that not every alleyway leads to a successful partnership, but each exploration contributes to the venture's growth.

The chapter delves into the ripple effects of successful collaborations. The reader is invited to witness scenes of joint projects taking shape, where the strengths of each partner complement the other. The city becomes a canvas for shared initiatives—events, workshops, and campaigns that emanate from the synergy of collaborative efforts. The impact extends beyond the venture, echoing through the urban landscape.

Scenes unfold where Mike, once navigating the entrepreneurial landscape alone, is now surrounded by a network of partners and collaborators. The vibrancy of the co-working space becomes a reflection of the diversity of skills and perspectives within this newfound ecosystem. The reader is drawn into the camaraderie as shared spaces become hubs of creativity and innovation.

The narrative explores the challenges inherent in managing multiple partnerships. Scenes depict Mike juggling the demands of collaboration, from coordinating timelines to navigating the intricacies of shared responsibilities. The city, depicted as a labyrinth of interconnected streets, becomes a metaphor for the delicate balance required to nurture and sustain these alliances.

As the chapter progresses, the narrative builds to a pivotal moment—a scene where Mike addresses the team in the wake of a successful partnership launch. The cityscape, now aglow with the lights of shared accomplishments, becomes a backdrop to his words of gratitude and encouragement. The speech marks not just a celebration of individual achievements but a recognition of the collective strength forged through strategic collaborations.

The chapter concludes with a sense of both reflection and anticipation. The city, depicted as a nexus of opportunity, stands as a silent witness to the ongoing dance of entrepreneurship. The reader is left on the edge of curiosity, eager to discover how these alliances and partnerships will shape the chapters that unfold in the evolving narrative of Mike's venture.

Chapter 12:

HARBINGERS OF PROGRESS

In the labyrinth of entrepreneurship, Chapter 12 unfolds with the signs of progress, small victories that illuminate the path forward for Mike and his venture. The cityscape, now a familiar backdrop, transforms with the dawn of achievements, becoming a canvas painted with the hues of success.

The narrative opens with scenes of reflection as Mike gazes at the city skyline from the window of his office. The structures that once seemed imposing now stand as symbols of resilience and determination. The chapter sets the tone with a sense of quiet anticipation, capturing the essence of a journey that is beginning to yield tangible results.

As the chapter progresses, the reader is led through key milestones that mark the venture's progression. Scenes unfold in the vibrant co-working space, where the hum of productivity becomes a testament to the collective efforts of the team. The city, depicted as a living organism, provides the soundtrack to scenes of collaboration, innovation, and the subtle markers of success.

The narrative delves into the quantitative and qualitative indicators of progress. Financial reports, once a source of anxiety, now reveal signs of stability and growth. The reader is led through scenes where the venture secures a larger client base, achieves higher revenue streams, and garners positive attention from industry insiders. The city, with its dynamic pulse, becomes a reflection of the venture's burgeoning success.

Scenes unfold where Mike and his team, once immersed in the struggles of the early stages, now find themselves navigating the challenges of scaling up. The narrative captures moments of strategic decision-making, from expanding the team to refining operational processes. The city, depicted as a sprawling landscape, becomes a metaphor for the expansive opportunities that emerge with the signs of progress.

The chapter explores the impact of success on team dynamics. Scenes depict the vibrancy of the co-working space, now teeming with a growing team of individuals united by a common vision. The camaraderie becomes palpable as shared achievements foster a sense of collective pride. The reader is drawn into the energy of the workspace, where every desk becomes a hub of innovation.

As the venture gains recognition, the narrative explores the changing external perceptions. Scenes unfold in industry events and conferences where Mike, once a newcomer, is now invited to speak and share insights. The city's event spaces become arenas for showcasing the venture's achievements, and the reader is led through moments of recognition that validate the progress made.

The chapter weaves in scenes of celebration, where milestones are marked not just with numbers on a balance sheet but with shared triumphs. Scenes unfold in rooftop gatherings and office parties where laughter and applause become the soundtrack to moments of acknowledgment. The city, now alive with the glow of celebration, stands witness to the joy that accompanies the signs of progress.

Amidst the achievements, the narrative doesn't shy away from the challenges that come with growth. Scenes depict late-night strategy sessions, where Mike and his team grapple with the complexities of scaling the venture. The city, depicted as a dynamic entity, becomes a metaphor for the ever-shifting landscape that requires constant adaptation and innovation.

The chapter explores moments of personal reflection for Mike. Scenes unfold where he revisits the initial business plan and goals set during the early days of the venture. The city, now a tapestry of memories, becomes a touchstone for measuring progress against the aspirations of the past. The reader is drawn into the introspection, witnessing the evolution of both the venture and its founder.

Intertwined with the quantitative indicators are scenes that delve into the qualitative aspects of success. Customer testimonials, positive reviews, and the impact of the venture on the lives of its users become harbingers of progress. The city, depicted in this light, becomes a community of interconnected individuals whose stories are woven into the fabric of the venture's success.

As the chapter reaches its climax, the narrative builds to a pivotal moment—a scene where Mike addresses the team amidst the backdrop of the city's skyline. The speech becomes a rallying cry, acknowledging the collective efforts that have led to the signs of progress. The city, now illuminated by the lights of accomplishment, stands as a silent witness to the shared triumphs of the entrepreneurial journey.

The chapter concludes with a sense of both reflection and anticipation. The city, depicted as a landscape transformed by the glow of success, stands as a testament to the resilience and determination that define the venture's progress. The reader is left on the edge of curiosity, eager to discover how these signs of progress will shape the unfolding chapters in the ongoing narrative of Mike's entrepreneurial journey.

Chapter 13:

THE BREAKTHROUGH HORIZON

In the saga of Mike's entrepreneurial odyssey, Chapter 13 dawns with the promise of a major breakthrough, a moment that casts a transformative light on the trajectory of his venture. The cityscape, bathed in the golden hues of dawn, becomes a canvas for the impending breakthrough, mirroring the anticipation that permeates the narrative.

The chapter opens with scenes of heightened anticipation as Mike navigates a pivotal meeting. The city, depicted as a bustling backdrop to the unfolding drama, sets the stage for a moment that holds the potential to redefine the venture's destiny. The reader is drawn into the tension, where each step Mike takes echoes with the weight of the breakthrough that hangs in the balance.

As the narrative unfolds, the reader is led through the intricate dance of negotiations and strategic discussions. Scenes transition between the sleek interiors of boardrooms and the vibrant co-working space, where the hum of productivity becomes a symphony of ambition. The city, with its skyscrapers reaching toward the heavens, becomes a metaphor for the limitless possibilities that a major breakthrough promises.

The narrative delves into the stakes at play—the potential client or partner whose involvement could catapult the venture to new heights. The city's skyline, visible through office windows, becomes a silent witness to the high-stakes conversations that will either mark the dawn of a breakthrough era or relegate the venture to the shadows of missed opportunities.

The chapter introduces key characters who play pivotal roles in this breakthrough narrative. Scenes unfold in coffee shops and collaborative spaces where Mike engages in discussions with industry influencers and decision-makers. The city's dynamic landscape becomes a backdrop for the intersections of networks, a meeting point where potential collaborators converge.

As the breakthrough moment inches closer, the narrative builds tension with scenes of meticulous preparation. Mike and his team refine pitches, rehearse presentations, and strategize every aspect of the impending breakthrough. The city, depicted in this phase as a labyrinth of possibilities, becomes a metaphor for the intricate web of details that must align for success.

The breakthrough itself unfolds in a climactic scene, set against the backdrop of a city skyline illuminated by the setting sun. The reader is led through moments of intense negotiation, where the weight of each word reverberates in the room. The city, now painted in the warm hues of twilight, becomes a metaphor for the transformative glow that bathes the venture in the wake of the breakthrough.

The narrative captures the emotional crescendo as the breakthrough is secured—a moment marked by handshakes, signed contracts, and a shared sense of achievement. Scenes unfold where the cityscape, visible through office windows, becomes a symbol of the venture's ascent to new heights. The reader is immersed in the euphoria, where every step resonates with the echoes of the breakthrough.

As the chapter progresses, the narrative explores the cascading impact of the breakthrough. Scenes unfold in the aftermath, where the city's event spaces become stages for celebrating the achievement. The reader is led through scenes of congratulatory toasts, shared laughter, and a sense of collective pride that permeates the vibrant co-working space.

The breakthrough becomes a catalyst for expansion and growth. Scenes depict the venture securing new clients, entering untapped markets, and garnering attention from industry publications. The city, depicted as an expansive landscape, becomes a metaphor for the boundless horizons that open up in the wake of the breakthrough.

The narrative delves into the personal growth that accompanies this transformative moment. Scenes unfold where Mike, once an entrepreneur navigating uncharted waters, now stands as a leader whose vision has been validated. The city, depicted as a symbol of both challenge and triumph, becomes a testament to the resilience and determination that define his journey.

Intertwined with the quantitative measures of success are scenes that explore the qualitative aspects of the breakthrough. Customer testimonials flood in, positive reviews become a chorus of acclaim, and the impact of the venture on its users reaches new heights. The city, depicted in this light, becomes a community of individuals whose lives have been touched by the breakthrough.

As the chapter reaches its climax, the narrative builds to a pivotal scene where Mike addresses the team against the backdrop of the city's illuminated skyline. The speech becomes a rallying cry, acknowledging the collective efforts that led to the breakthrough. The city, now aglow with the lights of accomplishment, stands as a silent witness to the shared triumphs of the entrepreneurial journey.

The chapter concludes with a sense of both reflection and anticipation. The city, transformed by the breakthrough, stands as a testament to the resilience and determination that define the venture's progress. The reader is left on the edge of curiosity, eager to discover how this major breakthrough will shape the unfolding chapters in the ongoing narrative of Mike's entrepreneurial journey.

Chapter 14:

CULTIVATING WISDOM, HARVESTING GROWTH

Amidst the triumphs and breakthroughs, Chapter 14 unfurls as a tapestry of personal growth and profound lessons for Mike. The cityscape, now a familiar companion in his journey, provides the backdrop for this chapter, where the skyscrapers stand as monuments to the heights he has reached and the wisdom cultivated along the way.

The narrative opens with scenes of reflection as Mike gazes out over the city from the vantage point of his office. The bustling streets below become a visual metaphor for the dynamic landscape of his own growth. The chapter sets the tone with a sense of introspection, capturing the essence of a leader who has weathered storms and emerged wiser on the other side.

As the chapter unfolds, the reader is led through the milestones that mark not just the venture's success but Mike's evolution as an entrepreneur and individual. Scenes transition between the vibrant co-working space and moments of solitude where he contemplates the journey thus far. The city, depicted as a repository of memories, becomes a testament to the transformative power of experience.

The narrative delves into the personal lessons learned, exploring moments of vulnerability and resilience. Scenes unfold where Mike grapples with the challenges of leadership, acknowledging that the path to success is paved with both triumphs and setbacks. The city, depicted as a symbol of both growth and stagnation, becomes a canvas for the complexities of the entrepreneurial journey.

The chapter explores the development of emotional intelligence as Mike navigates the interpersonal dynamics of leadership. Scenes depict moments of empathy and understanding as he learns to balance the needs of the team with the demands of the venture. The city's diverse population becomes a metaphor for the myriad personalities within the workspace, each requiring a unique approach.

The narrative weaves in scenes of mentorship, where Mike seeks guidance from seasoned entrepreneurs who have traversed similar paths. Coffee shop meetings and shared moments of reflection become windows into the collective wisdom of those who have weathered the storms of entrepreneurship. The city, depicted as a hub of knowledge exchange, becomes a source of inspiration and guidance.

As the venture grows, the chapter explores the challenges of scaling leadership. Scenes unfold where Mike grapples with delegation, learning to trust his team and empower them to take on greater responsibilities. The city, depicted as a labyrinth of possibilities, becomes a metaphor for the intricacies of managing a growing enterprise.

The narrative delves into the importance of adaptability as Mike faces the ever-evolving landscape of the business world. Scenes depict him navigating market shifts, technological advancements, and changing consumer behaviors. The city, with its fluidity and dynamism, becomes a reflection of the flexibility required to stay ahead in a competitive environment.

The chapter explores the integration of work and life as Mike strives to find balance amidst the demands of entrepreneurship. Scenes unfold where he carves out moments for family, acknowledging the importance of maintaining personal connections in the face of professional challenges. The city, depicted as a space for both work and leisure, becomes a metaphor for the delicate equilibrium he seeks.

Intertwined with the personal growth are scenes that explore the impact of success on Mike's mindset. The once-driven entrepreneur, focused solely on overcoming challenges, now finds moments to celebrate achievements and savor the journey. Scenes unfold where he embraces a mindset of abundance, acknowledging the positive impact of the venture on his life and the lives of those around him.

The narrative unfolds as Mike becomes a beacon of inspiration within the entrepreneurial community. Scenes depict him speaking at events and conferences, sharing insights and lessons from his journey. The city, now a stage for his influence, becomes a testament to the ripple effect of personal growth on the broader landscape of entrepreneurship.

As the chapter reaches its climax, the narrative builds to a pivotal moment—a scene where Mike addresses the team in a reflective meeting. The city's skyline, visible through office windows, becomes a backdrop to his words of gratitude and encouragement. The speech marks not just a celebration of individual and collective achievements but a recognition of the profound lessons learned along the way.

The chapter concludes with a sense of both reflection and anticipation. The city, standing as a silent witness to the evolution of Mike and his venture, becomes a symbol of growth and transformation. The reader is left on the edge of curiosity, eager to discover how the wisdom cultivated and lessons learned will shape the chapters that unfold in the ongoing narrative of Mike's entrepreneurial journey.

Chapter 15:

NAVIGATING THE UNEXPECTED STORMS

In the labyrinth of entrepreneurship, where success and challenge intertwine, Chapter 15 emerges as a testament to resilience as unexpected obstacles threaten the hard-won progress of Mike's venture. The cityscape, once a symbol of triumph, now becomes a canvas for navigating storms that cast shadows on the path forward.

The chapter unfolds with scenes of anticipation, where the city's skyline looms as both a fortress and a battleground. The narrative captures the tension that permeates the vibrant co-working space as the unexpected hurdles begin to materialize. The city, depicted as a dynamic and unpredictable force, sets the stage for a chapter defined by the trials that await.

As the narrative progresses, the reader is led through the unveiling of unexpected obstacles—market shifts, unforeseen competition, and technological disruptions that threaten the stability Mike and his team have worked so hard to establish. Scenes transition between crisis meetings within the co-working space and moments of introspection where Mike grapples with the weight of unforeseen challenges.

The city, once a symbol of boundless opportunity, becomes a backdrop for scenes of uncertainty. Coffee shops, once buzzing with the hum of creativity, now host strategizing sessions as the team faces the unexpected storms head-on. The once-familiar streets transform into a labyrinth of ambiguity, mirroring the complexity of the obstacles that have emerged.

The narrative explores the emotional toll of facing unexpected challenges. Scenes unfold where the once-confident team grapples with uncertainty and doubt. The city, depicted in this light, becomes a reflection of the shifting moods within the co-working space—moments of tension followed by the quiet determination to weather the storms.

As the unexpected obstacles manifest, the chapter delves into the tactical responses of Mike and his team. Scenes depict them reassessing strategies, reevaluating market dynamics, and pivoting in response to the unexpected shifts. The city, portrayed as a testing ground for adaptability, becomes a metaphor for the necessity of recalibrating in the face of unforeseen hurdles.

The narrative explores the external pressures that intensify as the unexpected storms persist. Scenes unfold in high-stakes negotiations and client meetings where the vulnerability of the venture is laid bare. The city's skyscrapers, once symbols of achievement, now loom as potential threats in the face of economic uncertainties and shifting industry landscapes.

The chapter introduces moments where unexpected obstacles have a cascading impact on the venture's financial stability. Scenes depict Mike and his team confronting the sobering reality of dwindling resources and the need to make difficult decisions. The city, with its juxtaposition of prosperity and challenges, becomes a reflection of the delicate balance required in navigating the storms of entrepreneurship.

Intertwined with the external challenges are scenes that delve into the strain on interpersonal relationships. The once-cohesive team faces the test of unity as unexpected obstacles strain their collective resolve. The city, depicted as a community within itself, becomes a backdrop for scenes of solidarity and moments of conflict as the team grapples with the storms that threaten their progress.

The narrative explores the impact on Mike's leadership as he navigates the unexpected storms. Scenes depict the weight of responsibility on his shoulders as he seeks to inspire confidence amidst uncertainty. The city, with its skyline standing as a silent witness, becomes a metaphor for the isolation that can accompany leadership in the face of unexpected challenges.

As the chapter unfolds, the narrative captures moments of resourcefulness and innovation. Scenes depict the team exploring alternative revenue streams, forging new partnerships, and leveraging their collective creativity to weather the storms. The city, depicted as a landscape of potential solutions, becomes a canvas for the entrepreneurial spirit to shine through adversity.

The chapter builds to a climactic scene—a moment where Mike addresses the team against the backdrop of the city's skyline. The speech becomes a rallying cry, acknowledging the unexpected obstacles while inspiring the team to face the challenges head-on. The city, now veiled in the shadows of uncertainty, stands as a silent witness to the resilience of the venture and its leader.

The chapter concludes with a sense of both reflection and anticipation. The city, now a landscape marked by the scars of unexpected storms, becomes a symbol of endurance. The reader is left on the edge of curiosity, eager to discover how Mike and his team will navigate the aftermath and reshape the narrative in the face of unexpected challenges.

Chapter 16:

CONFRONTING SHADOWS OF DOUBT

In the ongoing saga of Mike's entrepreneurial journey, Chapter 16 unfolds as a deeply introspective narrative, where he confronts the shadows of doubt that threaten to eclipse the progress of his venture. The cityscape, once a canvas of triumphs, now stands as a backdrop for the internal struggles that define this chapter.

The narrative opens with scenes of contemplation as Mike gazes out over the city from his office window. The skyline, once a symbol of aspiration, now casts long shadows that mirror the doubts creeping into his mind. The chapter sets the tone with a sense of vulnerability, capturing the internal turbulence that accompanies unexpected challenges.

As the chapter progresses, the reader is led through the labyrinth of Mike's thoughts—a landscape marked by uncertainty, fear, and the gnawing presence of doubt. Scenes transition between the vibrant co-working space and moments of solitude where Mike grapples with the weight of the unexpected storms. The city, depicted as a reflection of his internal landscape, becomes a metaphor for the shadows that loom within.

The narrative delves into the fear that takes root as Mike confronts the harsh realities of entrepreneurship. Scenes unfold where he revisits the initial dreams that fueled his venture, questioning whether the journey is still worth the sacrifices. The city, once a beacon of opportunity, becomes a place of internal conflict as Mike navigates the intersection of passion and doubt.

As the shadows of doubt intensify, the chapter explores the impact on Mike's confidence and decision-making. Scenes depict moments of hesitancy as he weighs strategic choices, grapples with the uncertainty of the market, and questions his ability to lead the venture through the storm. The city, with its ever-changing dynamics, becomes a mirror reflecting the shifting tides of his confidence.

The narrative introduces moments of self-reflection where Mike confronts his own vulnerabilities. Scenes unfold in coffee shops and late-night walks through the city, where he wrestles with the fear of failure and the weight of responsibility. The city's streets, once pathways of ambition, become a maze of introspection as he navigates the internal landscape of doubt.

The chapter explores the strains on personal relationships as Mike confronts the shadows of doubt. Scenes depict moments of tension as he grapples with the delicate balance between work and life. The city, depicted as a space where both personal and professional spheres converge, becomes a reflection of the complexities that arise when doubts cast their shadows over one's journey.

Intertwined with the internal struggles are scenes that delve into the support system around Mike. The vibrant co-working space becomes a microcosm of encouragement, with team members offering words of reassurance and shared determination. The city, depicted as a community within itself, becomes a backdrop for scenes of solidarity as the team faces the collective challenge of confronting doubt.

As the narrative unfolds, the chapter captures moments of vulnerability that become catalysts for personal growth. Scenes depict Mike seeking advice from mentors, engaging in candid conversations with the team, and acknowledging that facing doubt is an integral part of the entrepreneurial journey. The city, depicted as a stage for growth, becomes a symbol of resilience as he confronts the shadows head-on.

The narrative explores the power of self-discovery as Mike grapples with doubt. Scenes unfold where he revisits past successes, drawing strength from the milestones achieved despite challenges. The city, with its landmarks serving as reminders of triumphs, becomes a backdrop for scenes of self-affirmation as he confronts the shadows with newfound resolve.

The chapter builds to a pivotal scene—a moment where Mike addresses the team amidst the backdrop of the city's skyline. The speech becomes a raw and honest acknowledgment of doubt, a rallying cry that transforms vulnerability into strength. The city, now illuminated by the lights of shared determination, stands as a testament to the resilience of both the venture and its leader.

The chapter concludes with a sense of both reflection and anticipation. The city, once shrouded in the shadows of doubt, becomes a landscape marked by the resilience of Mike and his team. The reader is left on the edge of

curiosity, eager to discover how this
confrontation with internal shadows will shape
the unfolding chapters in the ongoing narrative
of Mike's entrepreneurial journey.

Chapter 17:

ADAPTING AMIDST THE SHIFTING SANDS

As Mike stands at the crossroads of uncertainty, Chapter 17 unfolds as a narrative of adaptability, where he grapples with the changing circumstances that have reshaped the landscape of his entrepreneurial journey. The cityscape, now a canvas of transition, becomes the backdrop for a chapter defined by the art of recalibration and resilience.

The narrative opens with scenes of Mike surveying the cityscape from his office window. The skyline, once a static symbol of ambition, now mirrors the fluidity of the entrepreneurial journey. The chapter sets the tone with a sense of contemplation, capturing the essence of a leader poised to navigate the shifting sands of circumstances.

As the chapter progresses, the reader is led through the evolution of the venture in response to external changes. Scenes transition between the vibrant co-working space, where the team huddles in strategic discussions, and moments of solitude where Mike formulates a roadmap for adaptation. The city, depicted as a living entity, becomes a metaphor for the dynamic forces at play.

The narrative delves into the impact of external factors—market trends, technological advancements, and unforeseen competition—that necessitate a recalibration of strategies. Scenes unfold where Mike, once anchored to a set course, navigates the shifting sands with a mindset of agility and innovation. The city, portrayed as a reflection of change, becomes a canvas for the evolving landscape of the venture.

The chapter explores the tactical responses employed by Mike and his team to adapt to the changing circumstances. Scenes depict brainstorming sessions, where the once-static business plans are dissected and reshaped. The city's streets, once familiar pathways, become avenues for exploration as the team seeks new opportunities amidst the shifting sands.

As the narrative unfolds, the chapter captures moments of resilience within the team. Scenes depict the collective spirit as the members confront challenges head-on, embracing the need for adaptation as an inherent part of the entrepreneurial journey. The city, depicted as a community within itself, becomes a backdrop for scenes of collaboration and shared determination.

The narrative introduces key moments of innovation and experimentation. Scenes unfold where Mike and his team explore new market segments, adopt cutting-edge technologies, and pivot aspects of their business model. The city,

depicted as an incubator of ideas, becomes a
symbol of the venture's ability to thrive amidst
the uncertainties of change.

Amidst the external shifts, the chapter delves
into the internal adjustments required within the
venture. Scenes depict the team adapting to new
roles, acquiring fresh skills, and embracing a
mindset of continuous learning. The city, with
its ever-evolving skyline, becomes a metaphor
for the ongoing transformation within the co-
working space.

The narrative explores the strains on leadership
as Mike adapts to the changing circumstances.
Scenes depict him navigating decision-making
in the face of ambiguity, fostering open
communication within the team, and embodying
the flexibility required to lead in dynamic
environments. The city, standing as a backdrop
to these moments, becomes a symbol of the
evolving leadership dynamics.

As the chapter progresses, the narrative captures moments where the venture's resilience is tested by unforeseen challenges. Scenes unfold where Mike, undeterred by setbacks, leads the team in adapting strategies and forging ahead. The city, depicted as a landscape of both obstacles and opportunities, becomes a testament to the determination that defines their journey.

The chapter introduces scenes of collaboration and strategic alliances formed amidst the changing circumstances. Coffee shop meetings and collaborative spaces become arenas for forging partnerships that amplify the venture's resilience. The city, depicted as a network of interconnected opportunities, becomes a backdrop for scenes of collective strength in the face of change.

As the narrative builds, the chapter unfolds to a climactic scene—a moment where Mike addresses the team amidst the backdrop of the city's evolving skyline. The speech becomes a rallying cry, acknowledging the challenges of adaptation while instilling confidence in the collective ability to navigate the shifting sands. The city, now aglow with the lights of shared determination, stands as a silent witness to the resilience of both the venture and its leader.

The chapter concludes with a sense of both reflection and anticipation. The city, transformed by the adaptive spirit of Mike and his team, becomes a symbol of endurance. The reader is left on the edge of curiosity, eager to discover how this adaptability will shape the unfolding chapters in the ongoing narrative of Mike's entrepreneurial journey amidst the ever-shifting circumstances.

Chapter 18:

EXPANDING HORIZONS: NETWORK AND CUSTOMER GROWTH

As the chapters unfold in Mike's entrepreneurial odyssey, Chapter 18 emerges as a narrative of expansion, where he strategically broadens both his network and customer base. The cityscape, a dynamic backdrop to his journey, transforms into a playground of possibilities, each street corner and networking event presenting opportunities for growth.

The narrative opens with scenes of anticipation as Mike steps into the vibrant pulse of the city's networking events. The skyline, aglow with the promise of new connections, sets the tone for a chapter marked by the art of building relationships and fostering customer growth. The chapter captures the energy of a leader on the cusp of expanding the horizons of his venture.

As the chapter unfolds, the reader is led through the intricacies of network expansion. Scenes transition between co-working spaces, industry conferences, and collaborative events where Mike navigates the diverse landscape of potential collaborators. The city, depicted as a hub of interconnected possibilities, becomes a metaphor for the expansive opportunities awaiting within his expanding network.

The narrative delves into the purposeful cultivation of relationships as Mike strategically engages with industry influencers, fellow entrepreneurs, and potential partners. Scenes unfold in crowded coffee shops and the dynamic backdrop of the city's skyline, each interaction becoming a brushstroke in the canvas of his expanding network. The city, a tapestry of connections, becomes a reflection of the growing web of relationships woven into the venture's journey.

The chapter explores the impact of digital platforms on network expansion. Scenes depict Mike leveraging social media, online forums, and digital communities to extend the reach of his network beyond geographical boundaries. The city, now interconnected through virtual spaces, becomes a symbol of the borderless opportunities unlocked by digital connectivity.

Intertwined with network expansion is the strategic growth of the customer base. Scenes unfold where Mike refines marketing strategies, taps into new demographics, and explores innovative channels to reach a wider audience. The city, depicted as a diverse landscape, becomes a metaphor for the myriad customer segments waiting to be discovered within its streets.

The narrative captures moments where the venture's value proposition resonates with new customers. Scenes unfold in storefronts and online platforms where the products or services gain traction, and the city becomes a living testament to the expanding footprint of the venture. Each transaction becomes a bridge connecting the venture to a growing community of customers.

As the chapter progresses, the narrative explores the challenges inherent in scaling customer growth. Scenes depict Mike and his team refining customer support systems, streamlining logistics, and innovating to meet the evolving needs of a larger customer base. The city, depicted as a bustling marketplace, becomes a metaphor for the dynamic environment where the venture's offerings find resonance.

The chapter delves into the personalized approach adopted by Mike to foster customer loyalty. Scenes unfold where he listens to customer feedback, responds to queries, and incorporates customer insights into the evolution of the venture. The city, with its diversity, becomes a metaphor for the individual voices within the collective chorus of customer experiences.

The narrative introduces scenes of strategic partnerships formed to enhance customer reach. Collaborations with influencers, cross-promotions with complementary businesses, and joint ventures become avenues for exponential growth. The city, depicted as a collaborative ecosystem, becomes a backdrop for scenes of synergy that amplify the venture's visibility.

Amidst the expansion, the chapter explores the impact on the internal dynamics of the venture. Scenes depict Mike leading a team that adapts to the demands of growth, from scaling production to enhancing customer service capabilities. The city's skyline, visible from office windows, becomes a symbol of both the challenges and triumphs embedded in the venture's journey.

The chapter builds to a climactic scene—a moment where Mike addresses the team amidst the backdrop of the city's expansive skyline. The speech becomes a celebration of collective achievements, acknowledging the growth of both the network and customer base. The city, now illuminated by the lights of shared success, stands as a testament to the resilience and adaptability of the venture.

The chapter concludes with a sense of both reflection and anticipation. The city, transformed by the expanding horizons of Mike's network and customer base, becomes a symbol of the ongoing journey. The reader is left on the edge of curiosity, eager to discover how these expansions will shape the unfolding chapters in the ongoing narrative of Mike's entrepreneurial voyage.

Chapter 19:

NAVIGATING THE ETHICAL CROSSROADS

In the tapestry of Mike's entrepreneurial narrative, Chapter 19 unfolds as a gripping exploration of ethical dilemmas and the tough decisions that accompany them. The cityscape, once a vibrant backdrop to his journey, becomes a complex maze of choices, each street corner presenting a moral crossroads that tests the very fabric of the venture.

The narrative opens with scenes of contemplation as Mike grapples with decisions that extend beyond the conventional metrics of success. The city, with its diverse communities and bustling streets, becomes a metaphor for the intricate web of ethical considerations that defines this chapter. The tone is set for a narrative marked by moral complexity and the weight of responsibility.

As the chapter progresses, the reader is led through moments where the venture faces ethical crossroads—decisions that stretch beyond profit margins and market share. Scenes transition between the co-working space and pivotal meetings where Mike and his team confront the moral implications of their choices. The city, depicted as a stage for ethical challenges, becomes a reflection of the conflicts that arise within the venture.

The narrative delves into the impact of these ethical dilemmas on the team dynamics. Scenes depict moments of heated discussions and introspective debates within the co-working space as individuals grapple with the moral implications of their actions. The city, with its diverse population, becomes a microcosm of perspectives that contribute to the complexity of ethical decision-making.

The chapter explores the external pressures that intensify ethical considerations. Scenes unfold in boardrooms and collaborative spaces where Mike negotiates deals, navigates partnerships, and faces situations where the moral compass of the venture is tested. The city's skyline, visible through office windows, becomes a silent witness to the high-stakes conversations that define these ethical crossroads.

Intertwined with the external challenges are scenes that delve into the internal moral compass of the venture. Mike, as the leader, grapples with the responsibility of making decisions that align with the ethical values he envisions for the venture. The city, depicted as a reflection of both opportunity and ethical quandaries, becomes a canvas for the evolving moral landscape of the entrepreneurial journey.

The narrative introduces moments where ethical considerations intersect with the venture's relationships with customers and stakeholders. Scenes depict Mike navigating transparency, honesty, and fair business practices as pillars of the venture's commitment to ethical entrepreneurship. The city, portrayed as a marketplace of integrity, becomes a testament to the enduring value of principled business decisions.

As the chapter unfolds, the narrative captures the personal toll of ethical dilemmas on Mike. Scenes unfold in coffee shops and contemplative walks through the city, where he grapples with the weight of decisions that extend beyond the bottom line. The city's streets, once pathways of ambition, become a labyrinth of introspection as he navigates the moral complexities of leadership.

The chapter explores moments where the venture faces public scrutiny, raising questions about the ethical integrity of its decisions. Scenes depict Mike addressing concerns from customers, stakeholders, and the broader community. The city, depicted as an arena of public perception, becomes a reflection of the consequences that ethical decisions can have on the venture's reputation.

The narrative introduces scenes of internal conflict within the team as individuals contend with differing ethical perspectives. Coffee shop meetings become forums for dialogue, where the diverse voices within the venture contribute to the ethical decision-making process. The city, with its cultural diversity, becomes a symbol of the myriad ethical viewpoints that shape the venture's choices.

Amidst the ethical challenges, the chapter explores moments of resilience and moral growth. Scenes depict Mike and his team recalibrating strategies, revisiting decisions, and adopting ethical frameworks that guide the venture toward a more principled path. The city, now a landscape marked by ethical introspection, becomes a testament to the transformative power of facing moral challenges head-on.

The chapter builds to a climactic scene—a moment where Mike addresses the team against the backdrop of the city's illuminated skyline. The speech becomes a reflection on the ethical journey undertaken, acknowledging the lessons learned and reaffirming the commitment to principled entrepreneurship. The city, now aglow with the lights of moral integrity, stands as a silent witness to the resilience and ethical evolution of the venture.

The chapter concludes with a sense of both reflection and anticipation. The city, transformed by the ethical choices made, becomes a symbol of enduring values. The reader is left on the edge of curiosity, eager to discover how the ethical compass of the venture will guide its path in the unfolding chapters of Mike's ongoing entrepreneurial voyage.

Chapter 20:

EARNING STRIPES: RECOGNITION AND RESPECT IN THE INDUSTRY

As the chapters of Mike's entrepreneurial saga unfold, Chapter 20 emerges as a crescendo, a narrative symphony resonating with the sweet melodies of recognition and respect within the industry. The cityscape, a witness to the highs and lows of his journey, transforms into a stage where the venture earns its stripes, standing tall amidst the giants of the business world.

The narrative opens with scenes of anticipation as Mike navigates industry events, conferences, and award ceremonies. The skyline, illuminated by the city lights, becomes a backdrop to moments where the venture steps into the spotlight, earning its place among industry leaders. The chapter sets the tone for a narrative marked by validation and the fruits of unwavering dedication.

As the chapter progresses, the reader is led through milestones that mark the ascent of the venture to industry prominence. Scenes transition between co-working spaces and prestigious events where Mike and his team showcase their achievements. The city, depicted as a landscape of recognition, becomes a metaphor for the expansive horizons unlocked by the venture's growing influence.

The narrative delves into the strategic initiatives that contribute to the venture's recognition. Scenes unfold where Mike refines marketing campaigns, establishes thought leadership, and positions the venture as a trailblazer within its niche. The city's streets, once avenues of opportunity, become pathways that lead the venture to the forefront of industry conversations.

The chapter explores the impact of innovative products, services, or business models that distinguish the venture within the competitive landscape. Scenes depict moments of breakthroughs and accolades, where the city's skyscrapers stand as metaphors for the heights reached by the venture's contributions. The city, now a symbol of industry excellence, becomes a testament to the transformative power of innovation.

Intertwined with industry recognition is the strategic cultivation of relationships with influencers and key players. Scenes unfold where Mike engages in partnerships, collaborates on industry initiatives, and solidifies the venture's presence within professional networks. The city, with its vibrant community, becomes a reflection of the alliances forged on the path to industry respect.

The narrative introduces scenes where the venture's leadership becomes synonymous with expertise and authority. Mike, now a sought-after speaker and commentator, contributes valuable insights to industry discussions. The city, depicted as a hub of knowledge exchange, becomes a backdrop for scenes where the venture's influence extends beyond its immediate circles.

Amidst the industry recognition, the chapter explores moments of validation from customers, stakeholders, and peers. Scenes depict testimonials, positive reviews, and collaborative testimonials that add layers to the venture's reputation. The city, now a living testament to the impact of the venture's offerings, becomes a symbol of the trust placed in its capabilities.

The narrative captures scenes of media coverage and industry features that amplify the venture's visibility. The city's billboards and digital screens become canvases for the venture's success stories, marking its ascent to industry acclaim. Each headline becomes a stroke in the portrait of recognition painted within the bustling cityscape.

As the chapter progresses, the narrative explores the internal dynamics within the team as they bask in the glow of industry recognition. Scenes depict moments of celebration, team-building events, and a shared sense of pride that permeates the co-working space. The city, now a stage for collective success, becomes a symbol of the collaborative efforts that led to industry acclaim.

The chapter builds to a climactic scene—a moment where Mike addresses the team amidst the backdrop of the city's illuminated skyline. The speech becomes a celebration of collective achievements, acknowledging the journey from humble beginnings to industry recognition. The city, now aglow with the lights of shared success, stands as a testament to the resilience and strategic prowess of the venture.

The chapter concludes with a sense of both reflection and anticipation. The city, transformed by the recognition and respect earned, becomes a symbol of enduring influence. The reader is left on the edge of curiosity, eager to discover how the venture will leverage this newfound status in the unfolding chapters of Mike's ongoing entrepreneurial voyage.

Chapter 21:

MILESTONES AND VICTORIES: CELEBRATING MAJOR SUCCESSES

In the vibrant tapestry of Mike's entrepreneurial narrative, Chapter 21 unfurls as a jubilant symphony—a celebration of major successes that punctuate the venture's journey. The cityscape, adorned with the glow of achievement, transforms into a stage where triumphs are not only acknowledged but reverberate as beacons of inspiration. It's a chapter marked by accomplishment, recognition, and the collective joy that comes with reaching significant milestones.

The narrative opens with scenes of anticipation, the city skyline adorned with lights that mirror the gleam of success. The once-ordinary streets now pulse with the energy of achievement. The chapter sets the stage for a narrative of celebration, where every success, no matter how incremental, becomes a cause for collective pride and revelry.

As the chapter unfolds, the reader is led through the tapestry of victories that grace the venture's path. Scenes transition between the co-working space, celebratory gatherings, and strategic meetings where Mike and his team reflect on the magnitude of their achievements. The city, now a canvas of triumph, becomes a metaphor for the dynamic landscape where the venture thrives.

The narrative delves into the milestones that mark the venture's ascent to success. Scenes unfold where product launches, market expansions, and strategic collaborations become the building blocks of the venture's triumph. The city's dynamic skyline, visible through office windows, becomes a reflection of the venture's growth and the evolving narrative of its success.

The chapter explores moments of customer appreciation and loyalty that amplify the venture's impact. Scenes depict Mike engaging with delighted customers, receiving positive testimonials, and leveraging feedback to enhance the venture's offerings. The city's streets, now pathways of endorsement, become avenues where the venture's success resonates with its audience.

Amidst the celebrations, the narrative captures scenes of team empowerment and camaraderie. Moments of recognition, team-building events, and shared successes become the threads weaving a tapestry of a workplace culture that fosters both individual and collective triumph. The city, now a hub of shared achievement, becomes a symbol of the venture's commitment to nurturing a team that thrives together.

The chapter unfolds scenes where the venture's financial health experiences buoyancy. Scenes depict Mike in discussions with stakeholders, investors, and financial analysts as the venture's profitability becomes a testament to its strategic acumen. The city's economic pulse, now intertwined with the venture's success, becomes a reflection of its financial ascent.

As the chapter progresses, the narrative unveils scenes of industry recognition and accolades. Scenes depict award ceremonies, media features, and industry events where Mike and his team stand as luminaries within their field. The city, with its billboards and digital screens, becomes a canvas for celebrating the venture's triumph in the broader community.

The chapter builds to a climactic scene—a moment where Mike addresses the team amidst the backdrop of the city's illuminated skyline. The speech becomes a celebration of collective triumph, an acknowledgment of the journey from humble beginnings to major successes, and a rallying cry for the continued pursuit of excellence. The city, now aglow with the lights of shared success, stands as a testament to the resilience, innovation, and unwavering determination that define the venture.

The narrative captures the essence of celebratory moments within the co-working space, where teams gather to toast to their accomplishments. Scenes unfold where the office becomes a hub of joy, laughter, and shared pride as the venture's major successes are recounted and celebrated. The city's energy, now a reflection of the venture's triumph, becomes intertwined with the festive spirit within the workplace.

As the celebration extends beyond the office walls, the narrative depicts scenes of community engagement. The venture's success becomes a source of inspiration, and scenes unfold where Mike and his team participate in community events, mentorship programs, and initiatives that give back to the city that has been a witness to their journey. The city, now a beneficiary of the venture's success, becomes a recipient of the goodwill fostered by the triumphs achieved.

The chapter concludes with a sense of both reflection and anticipation. The city, transformed by the celebration of major successes, becomes a symbol of enduring influence. The reader is left on the edge of curiosity, eager to discover how the venture will leverage these triumphs in the unfolding chapters of Mike's ongoing entrepreneurial voyage.

Chapter 22:

NAVIGATING NEW WATERS: CHALLENGES AND COMPETITION

In the ever-evolving journey of Mike's entrepreneurial odyssey, Chapter 22 unfurls as a narrative of transition, where the venture encounters new challenges and faces heightened competition. The cityscape, once a familiar backdrop to triumphs, transforms into a dynamic arena where uncharted waters bring forth tests of resilience and strategic ingenuity.

The narrative opens with scenes of anticipation as Mike surveys the shifting landscape of the industry. The skyline, now punctuated with new players and challenges, becomes a canvas for the venture's next chapter. The chapter sets the tone for a narrative marked by uncertainty, where each corner turned within the city holds the potential for both obstacles and opportunities.

As the chapter progresses, the reader is led through the unveiling of new challenges that arise within the venture's path. Scenes transition between the co-working space and strategic meetings where Mike and his team analyze the complexities of the evolving industry. The city, depicted as a reflection of the competitive landscape, becomes a metaphor for the unexplored territories that lie ahead.

The narrative delves into the impact of shifting market dynamics, technological advancements, and emerging trends that disrupt the status quo. Scenes unfold where Mike navigates through data analytics, market research, and scenario planning to gain insights into the challenges posed by the evolving industry. The city, with its ever-changing skyline, becomes a symbol of the dynamic forces at play.

The chapter explores the introduction of new competitors, both emerging startups and established players seeking to expand their reach. Scenes depict strategic analyses and competitive assessments within the co-working space, where Mike and his team evaluate the strengths and weaknesses of these new entrants. The city, a marketplace of ideas and innovation, becomes a reflection of the intensified competition within the industry.

Amidst the new challenges, the narrative captures moments where the venture must reassess its positioning and adapt to the evolving market landscape. Scenes unfold where Mike refines marketing strategies, explores product innovations, and seeks to differentiate the venture within the face of increased competition. The city, now a proving ground for strategic agility, becomes a metaphor for the adaptability required to navigate uncharted waters.

The chapter explores the internal dynamics within the team as they confront the pressures of heightened competition. Scenes depict moments of brainstorming, collaboration, and a collective determination to rise to the challenges posed by new entrants. The city, with its diverse population, becomes a microcosm of the collaborative spirit needed to navigate through uncharted waters.

The narrative introduces scenes where customer expectations undergo shifts, influenced by the offerings of competitors and changing industry standards. Scenes depict Mike engaging in customer feedback sessions, conducting surveys, and leveraging customer insights to align the venture with evolving preferences. The city, depicted as a hub of consumer activity, becomes a reflection of the dynamic demands shaping the competitive landscape.

As the chapter unfolds, the narrative captures moments where the venture faces external pressures, from economic fluctuations to regulatory changes that add layers of complexity to the entrepreneurial journey. Scenes depict

Mike in negotiations, legal consultations, and boardroom discussions where the venture's resilience is tested by the external forces at play. The city, now a tapestry of challenges, becomes a symbol of the multifaceted obstacles encountered within the evolving industry.

The chapter explores the impact of new challenges on the leadership dynamics within the venture. Scenes depict Mike navigating decision-making, fostering resilience within the team, and embodying the adaptability required to steer through uncharted waters. The city's skyline, visible through office windows, becomes a silent witness to the evolving leadership dynamics within the co-working space.

Amidst the challenges, the narrative introduces scenes of strategic alliances formed to strengthen the venture's position in the face of heightened competition. Collaborations with complementary businesses, joint ventures, and partnerships become avenues for mutual growth and resilience. The city, depicted as a network of interconnected opportunities, becomes a backdrop for scenes of collaborative strength amidst the evolving industry landscape.

The chapter builds to a climactic scene—a moment where Mike addresses the team amidst the backdrop of the city's dynamic skyline. The speech becomes a rallying cry, acknowledging the new challenges and intensified competition while instilling confidence in the collective ability to navigate uncharted waters. The city, now aglow with the lights of shared determination, stands as a testament to the resilience and strategic acumen of the venture.

The chapter concludes with a sense of both reflection and anticipation. The city, transformed by the challenges faced and strategic adaptations made, becomes a symbol of endurance. The reader is left on the edge of curiosity, eager to discover how the venture will navigate the uncharted waters and carve its path in the

unfolding chapters of Mike's ongoing
entrepreneurial journey.

Chapter 23:

STRAINED BONDS: PERSONAL RELATIONSHIPS UNDER PRESSURE

In the intricate tapestry of Mike's entrepreneurial narrative, Chapter 23 unfurls as a poignant exploration of the toll entrepreneurship takes on personal relationships. The cityscape, once a backdrop to triumphs and aspirations, transforms into a silent witness to the strains that emerge as the pressures of the entrepreneurial journey intensify.

The narrative opens with scenes of contrast, juxtaposing the bustling city streets with the personal spaces where Mike grapples with the demands of his venture. The skyline, now a shadowed silhouette against the city lights, sets the tone for a chapter marked by the complexities of balancing professional ambitions with personal connections. It's a narrative that delves into the inherent tensions that arise when the pursuit of dreams collides with the intricacies of human relationships.

As the chapter progresses, the reader is led through moments where the demands of entrepreneurship cast shadows on Mike's personal life. Scenes transition between boardroom discussions, late-night strategy sessions, and the intimate spaces where personal relationships navigate the ebb and flow of the entrepreneurial tide. The city, with its vibrant energy, becomes a backdrop for the unfolding dynamics of Mike's personal world.

The narrative delves into the impact of time constraints on Mike's availability for his loved ones. Scenes unfold where family dinners become interrupted by urgent calls, and personal commitments take a backseat to the demands of the venture. The city's streets, once pathways of connection, become avenues where the tension between professional obligations and personal time manifests.

The chapter explores moments of emotional strain as personal relationships bear the weight of the entrepreneur's responsibilities. Scenes depict intimate conversations fraught with the challenges of balancing priorities, where the city's skyline becomes a metaphor for the line between personal and professional realms blurring. The city, with its myriad stories, becomes a reflection of the intricate narratives woven into the fabric of personal connections.

Amidst the pressures, the narrative captures scenes where personal milestones and celebrations are overshadowed by the demands of the venture. Family birthdays, anniversaries, and special occasions become moments tinged with the awareness of absent presence. The city, with its celebration of life, becomes a poignant backdrop to scenes where personal joys are tempered by the strains of entrepreneurship.

The chapter explores the emotional toll on Mike as he grapples with the guilt of being physically present but mentally preoccupied. Scenes unfold where he navigates the delicate balance between being emotionally available to his loved ones and fulfilling the relentless demands of the venture. The city's lights, now distant beacons, become symbols of the emotional distance that emerges under the pressure of entrepreneurship.

The narrative introduces moments where personal relationships are tested by the uncertainties and setbacks inherent in the entrepreneurial journey. Scenes depict scenes of support, understanding, and resilience, but also moments of frustration, misunderstandings, and the strain of unmet expectations. The city, with its evolving dynamics, becomes a reflection of the fluidity of personal connections in the face of entrepreneurial challenges.

Amidst the emotional strains, the chapter explores the impact on Mike's own well-being as he navigates the intricate dance between personal and professional fulfillment. Scenes depict late-night reflections in the glow of the city lights, where he grapples with the toll entrepreneurship takes on his own mental and emotional resilience. The city, depicted as a beacon of both ambition and introspection, becomes a metaphor for the internal landscape of an entrepreneur under pressure.

As the chapter progresses, the narrative captures scenes of resilience within personal relationships. Moments of open communication, shared aspirations, and mutual support become beacons of hope amidst the challenges. The city's streets, now pathways of understanding, become avenues where personal bonds withstand the pressures of entrepreneurship.

The chapter builds to a climactic scene—a moment where Mike confronts the strains on personal relationships amidst the backdrop of the city's illuminated skyline. The reflection becomes a raw acknowledgment of the toll taken, a pledge to seek balance, and a commitment to nurturing personal connections amidst the relentless pace of entrepreneurship. The city, now aglow with the lights of shared understanding, stands as a testament to the resilience of personal relationships in the face of entrepreneurial pressures.

The chapter concludes with a sense of both reflection and anticipation. The city, transformed by the strains and resolutions within personal relationships, becomes a symbol of the intricate dance between personal and professional spheres. The reader is left on the edge of curiosity, eager to discover how Mike will navigate the delicate balance in the unfolding chapters of his ongoing entrepreneurial voyage.

Chapter 24:

TRIALS OF TENACITY: MIKE'S RESILIENCE TESTED

In the labyrinth of Mike's entrepreneurial journey, Chapter 24 emerges as a crucible, a narrative where his resilience faces rigorous testing. The cityscape, witness to the highs and lows, transforms into a theater of challenges that threaten to unravel the very fabric of the venture. It's a chapter marked by adversity, a testament to the mettle of an entrepreneur when confronted with the trials of tenacity.

The narrative opens with scenes of anticipation, the city skyline looming against a backdrop of uncertainty. The lights, once symbols of ambition, now cast long shadows that herald the tribulations ahead. The chapter sets the tone for a narrative marked by resilience pushed to its limits, where each corner turned within the city becomes a battleground for Mike's unyielding determination.

As the chapter progresses, the reader is led through a series of challenges that assail the venture from various fronts. Scenes transition between the co-working space, crisis meetings, and pivotal decisions where Mike and his team confront unforeseen obstacles. The city, depicted as a landscape of adversity, becomes a metaphor for the terrain where resilience will be tested.

The narrative delves into financial pressures that cast a shadow over the venture. Scenes unfold where revenue projections falter, funding sources dwindle, and the city's streets become pathways where the fiscal health of the venture faces its most formidable challenge. The city's skyline, once a beacon of possibilities, becomes a looming reminder of the financial cliffs that must be navigated.

The chapter explores moments where key partnerships fracture, alliances dissolve, and the once-steady ground beneath the venture's feet becomes shaky. Scenes depict Mike in negotiations, crisis talks, and intense strategizing sessions as he grapples with the complexities of salvaging crucial relationships. The city, with its interconnected web, becomes a metaphor for the delicate ties that bind the venture to its collaborators.

Amidst the external pressures, the narrative captures scenes of internal challenges as team morale wavers under the weight of adversity. Scenes unfold where the co-working space becomes a crucible of emotions, a place where resilience is not only an individual endeavor but a collective pursuit. The city, with its dynamic pulse, becomes a backdrop for scenes of shared determination in the face of tribulations.

The chapter explores moments where the market dynamics shift unexpectedly, presenting challenges that demand swift adaptability.

Scenes depict Mike and his team recalibrating strategies, reimagining products, and pivoting in response to the turbulent currents of the industry. The city, a theater of change, becomes a reflection of the evolving landscape where resilience becomes synonymous with adaptability.

The narrative introduces scenes where public perception becomes a battleground, with the venture grappling with reputational challenges and communication crises. Scenes unfold where Mike addresses the media, engages in damage control, and navigates the treacherous waters of public opinion. The city's billboards, once adorned with success stories, become spaces where the narrative of resilience is now rewritten.

Amidst the trials, the chapter explores the toll on Mike's mental and emotional well-being. Scenes depict late-night reflections in the glow of the city lights, where he confronts doubts, wrestles with anxiety, and summons the strength to endure. The city, depicted as both adversary and ally, becomes a mirror to the internal struggles that define the journey of an entrepreneur tested by adversity.

As the chapter progresses, the narrative captures moments of strategic innovation and bold decision-making. Scenes unfold where Mike leverages adversity as a crucible for creativity, where the city's streets become a canvas for the entrepreneurial spirit to redefine the narrative in the face of challenges. Resilience, now a beacon of hope, becomes a rallying cry amidst the turmoil.

The chapter builds to a climactic scene—a moment where Mike addresses the team amidst the backdrop of the city's illuminated skyline. The speech becomes a testament to the resilience forged in the crucible of adversity, an acknowledgment of the challenges faced, and a rallying cry for collective perseverance. The city, now aglow with the lights of shared determination, stands as a testament to the unyielding spirit that defines the venture.

The chapter concludes with a sense of both reflection and anticipation. The city, transformed by the resilience tested and triumphs achieved, becomes a symbol of endurance. The reader is left on the edge of curiosity, eager to discover how this resilience will shape the unfolding chapters in the ongoing narrative of Mike's entrepreneurial voyage.

Chapter 25:

CLIMAX: MIKE FACES THE BIGGEST CHALLENGE YET

In the grand tapestry of Mike's entrepreneurial saga, Chapter 25 unravels as the climactic pinnacle—a narrative where the protagonist confronts the most formidable challenge of his journey. The cityscape, a silent witness to triumphs and tribulations, transforms into an arena where the magnitude of adversity threatens to eclipse the very essence of the venture. It's a chapter marked by tension, resilience, and the defining moments that will shape the trajectory of Mike's entrepreneurial legacy.

The narrative opens with scenes of foreboding, the city skyline cast in shadows against the backdrop of a brooding sky. The lights, once vibrant symbols of possibility, now flicker in the

face of the impending challenge. The chapter
sets the stage for a narrative of epic proportions,
where the stakes are higher, the conflicts more
intense, and every decision made within the
city's confines resonates with consequence.

As the chapter unfolds, the reader is led through
the gradual revelation of the monumental
challenge that stands before the venture. Scenes
transition between the co-working space,
strategy sessions, and crucial meetings where
Mike and his team grapple with the intricacies of
the impending crisis. The city, now a labyrinth
of uncertainty, becomes a metaphor for the
uncharted territory where the venture's fate
hangs in the balance.

The narrative delves into the multifaceted nature
of the challenge—an amalgamation of financial
intricacies, market dynamics, and internal strains
that converge to create a perfect storm. Scenes
unfold where the co-working space becomes a
war room, a place where charts, graphs, and
projections map out the contours of the

monumental challenge. The city's skyline, visible through office windows, becomes a silent witness to the gravity of the situation.

The chapter explores the external pressures that compound the challenge—a confluence of economic shifts, industry disruptions, and unforeseen obstacles that intensify the complexity of the venture's predicament. Scenes depict Mike in negotiations, crisis talks, and strategic planning sessions where every decision made reverberates within the tumultuous landscape of the city. The city, with its diverse neighborhoods, becomes a tapestry where external forces entwine with the venture's destiny.

Amidst the challenges, the narrative captures moments of internal conflict as the team grapples with the enormity of the situation. Scenes unfold where the co-working space becomes an emotional battleground, a place where the resilience of each team member is tested amidst the mounting pressure. The city's streets, once avenues of possibility, become pathways where the venture's collective determination must navigate through the storm.

The chapter explores the impact on Mike's leadership as he navigates the uncharted waters of the biggest challenge yet. Scenes depict him at the forefront of decision-making, a captain steering the ship through turbulent seas. The city's skyline, now a symbol of both challenge and opportunity, becomes a reflection of the leadership qualities required to weather the impending storm.

The narrative introduces scenes of strategic innovation and unconventional solutions as Mike and his team seek to redefine the narrative amidst the crisis. Scenes unfold where the city becomes a canvas for creative problem-solving, where bold decisions and unorthodox approaches become the instruments to navigate through the challenge. The city, now a testing ground for ingenuity, becomes a metaphor for the transformative power of innovative thinking.

Amidst the turmoil, the chapter captures moments of personal sacrifice as Mike confronts the toll the challenge takes on his own well-being. Scenes depict late-night reflections in the glow of the city lights, where he grapples with doubts, wrestles with anxiety, and summons the strength to endure. The city, depicted as both adversary and ally, becomes a mirror to the internal struggles that define the journey of an entrepreneur facing the biggest challenge of his career.

As the chapter progresses, the narrative unfolds scenes of alliances formed and partnerships strengthened in the crucible of the challenge. Collaborations with industry peers, strategic alliances, and mutual support systems become beacons of hope amidst the chaos. The city's dynamic pulse, now a symphony of collaborative endeavors, becomes a backdrop for scenes where collective resilience becomes the key to overcoming the challenge.

The chapter builds to a climactic scene—a moment where Mike addresses the team amidst the backdrop of the city's illuminated skyline. The speech becomes a rallying cry, an acknowledgment of the magnitude of the challenge, and a call to collective resilience. The city, now aglow with the lights of shared determination, stands as a testament to the unwavering spirit that defines the venture in the face of its greatest trial.

The chapter concludes with a sense of both resolution and anticipation. The city, transformed by the resilience displayed and decisions made, becomes a symbol of endurance. The reader is left on the edge of curiosity, eager to discover how the venture will emerge from the crucible of the biggest challenge yet in the unfolding chapters of Mike's ongoing entrepreneurial voyage.

Chapter 26:

TRIUMPH OF RESOLVE: OVERCOMING CONFLICTS AND OBSTACLES

In the resounding echoes of the entrepreneurial journey, Chapter 26 emerges as a testament to the indomitable spirit—the narrative where conflicts are resolved, obstacles are dismantled, and the venture stands on the precipice of triumph. The cityscape, a witness to the venture's struggles and triumphs, transforms into a stage where resilience, strategic acumen, and unwavering determination take center stage.

The narrative opens with scenes of tension dissipating, the city skyline bathed in the glow of opportunity. The lights, once dimmed by conflict, now shine brighter against the canvas of

urban possibilities. The chapter sets the tone for
a narrative marked by resolution, where every
conflict resolved becomes a stepping stone
toward the summit of success.

As the chapter unfolds, the reader is led through
the gradual unravelling of conflicts that once
entangled the venture. Scenes transition between
the co-working space, collaborative meetings,
and reconciliatory discussions where Mike and
his team address the intricacies of internal
disputes. The city, now a symbol of unity,
becomes a metaphor for the shared journey of
overcoming conflicts within the venture.

The narrative delves into the transformative
power of open communication and
understanding as team members navigate
through past grievances. Scenes depict the co-
working space becoming a forum for dialogue,
where perspectives are shared, grievances aired,
and resolutions sought. The city's streets, once
pathways of discord, become avenues where the

venture's collective resilience paves the way for harmonious collaboration.

The chapter explores the impact of strategic decisions and compromises that contribute to the resolution of conflicts. Scenes unfold where Mike, as the leader, navigates negotiations, implements organizational changes, and fosters an environment conducive to reconciliation. The city's dynamic skyline, visible through office windows, becomes a silent witness to the structural shifts within the venture that pave the way for conflict resolution.

Amidst the internal reconciliation, the narrative captures scenes where external conflicts are addressed with strategic finesse. Scenes unfold where partnerships are mended, negotiations are successfully navigated, and the venture re-establishes itself within the intricate web of industry collaborations. The city, with its diverse ecosystems, becomes a reflection of the external alliances forged in the aftermath of conflict resolution.

The chapter explores moments of strategic innovation as the venture redefines its trajectory in the aftermath of conflict resolution. Scenes depict Mike and his team exploring new market opportunities, refining products, and leveraging the lessons learned from internal conflicts to drive external success. The city, now a canvas for creative resurgence, becomes a metaphor for the venture's ability to transform challenges into opportunities.

The narrative introduces scenes where individual team members experience personal growth as a result of conflict resolution. Professional development initiatives, mentorship programs, and collaborative projects become vehicles for skill enhancement and personal fulfillment. The city, depicted as a hub of growth, becomes a backdrop for scenes of individual triumphs within the venture.

Amidst the triumphs, the chapter captures moments of celebration within the co-working space. Scenes depict team-building events, shared victories, and a renewed sense of camaraderie that permeates the workplace. The city, now a hub of shared success, becomes a symbol of the collective triumph that arises when conflicts are resolved and obstacles overcome.

The chapter explores the impact on the venture's reputation and public perception as conflicts are resolved. Scenes depict Mike addressing stakeholders, communicating transparently, and steering the narrative of the venture toward one of resilience and growth. The city's billboards and digital screens become spaces where the triumph of resolve is broadcast to the broader community.

As the chapter progresses, the narrative unfolds scenes of renewed focus and determination within the team. Moments of strategic planning, goal-setting, and collaborative initiatives become the building blocks for the venture's resurgence. The city's streets, now pathways of purpose, become avenues where the triumph of resolve leads the venture toward new horizons.

The chapter builds to a climactic scene—a moment where Mike addresses the team amidst the backdrop of the city's illuminated skyline. The speech becomes a celebration of collective triumph, an acknowledgment of conflicts resolved, and a rallying cry for the continued pursuit of success. The city, now aglow with the lights of shared determination, stands as a testament to the resilience and unity that define the venture in the aftermath of conflict resolution.

The chapter concludes with a sense of both reflection and anticipation. The city, transformed by the triumph of resolve, becomes a symbol of endurance. The reader is left on the edge of curiosity, eager to discover how the venture will leverage this newfound unity in the unfolding chapters of Mike's ongoing entrepreneurial voyage.

Chapter 27:

TRIUMPH OF TENACITY: MIKE'S BUSINESS NOT ONLY SURVIVES BUT THRIVES

In the unfolding narrative of Mike's entrepreneurial saga, Chapter 27 emerges as a crescendo—a celebration of resilience, strategic acumen, and unwavering determination. The cityscape, a silent witness to the venture's evolution, transforms into a testament of triumph as Mike's business not only survives the challenges but thrives in the face of adversity. It's a chapter marked by renewal, growth, and the realization of the venture's fullest potential.

The narrative opens with scenes of transformation, the city skyline aglow with the vibrant lights of success. The once-muted skyline now stands as a testament to the resurgence of the venture, where every setback becomes a stepping stone toward unprecedented heights. The chapter sets the tone for a narrative marked by triumph, where the venture not only weathers the storm but emerges stronger on the other side.

As the chapter unfolds, the reader is led through the stages of revival within the venture. Scenes transition between the co-working space, strategic planning sessions, and celebratory gatherings where Mike and his team chart the trajectory of the venture's newfound success. The city, now a canvas of opportunity, becomes a metaphor for the dynamic landscape where the venture thrives.

The narrative delves into the strategic decisions that contribute to the venture's resurgence. Scenes unfold where Mike, as the visionary leader, leverages lessons learned from past challenges, refines business models, and explores innovative strategies that align with evolving market dynamics. The city's dynamic skyline, visible through office windows, becomes a reflection of the venture's adaptability and strategic agility.

The chapter explores moments of product innovation and service refinement that position the venture as a trailblazer within its industry. Scenes depict the co-working space becoming a hub of creativity, where teams collaborate on groundbreaking projects and ventures into uncharted territories. The city, depicted as a hub of innovation, becomes a symbol of the venture's commitment to pushing boundaries.

Amidst the revival, the narrative captures scenes of market expansion as the venture gains a stronger foothold in existing markets and explores new territories. Scenes unfold where Mike and his team embark on strategic partnerships, alliances, and marketing campaigns that amplify the venture's reach. The city's streets, now pathways of growth, become avenues where the venture extends its influence.

The chapter explores the impact of customer satisfaction and loyalty as the venture redefines its relationship with its audience. Scenes depict Mike engaging with customers, collecting feedback, and implementing improvements that resonate with the evolving needs of the market. The city, with its diverse population, becomes a reflection of the venture's ability to connect with and serve a broad audience.

Amidst the triumph, the narrative captures scenes of team empowerment and professional development. Moments of recognition, training programs, and shared successes become the building blocks for a workplace culture where every team member is a contributor to the venture's thriving narrative. The city, now a hub of collective achievement, becomes a symbol of the venture's commitment to nurturing its greatest asset—its people.

The chapter unfolds scenes where the venture's financial health not only stabilizes but experiences unprecedented growth. Scenes depict Mike in discussions with investors, securing funding, and navigating the financial landscape with strategic finesse. The city's skyscrapers, once distant aspirations, become symbols of the venture's ascent to new financial heights.

As the chapter progresses, the narrative unfolds moments where the venture gains industry recognition and accolades. Scenes depict award ceremonies, media features, and industry events where Mike and his team stand as exemplars of entrepreneurial success. The city, with its billboards and digital screens, becomes a canvas for celebrating the venture's triumph in the public eye.

The chapter builds to a climactic scene—a moment where Mike addresses the team amidst the backdrop of the city's illuminated skyline. The speech becomes a celebration of collective triumph, an acknowledgment of the journey from survival to thriving, and a rallying cry for the continued pursuit of excellence. The city, now aglow with the lights of shared success, stands as a testament to the resilience, innovation, and unwavering determination that define the venture.

The chapter concludes with a sense of both reflection and anticipation. The city, transformed by the venture's thriving narrative, becomes a symbol of enduring influence. The reader is left on the edge of curiosity, eager to discover how the venture will leverage its newfound success in the unfolding chapters of Mike's ongoing entrepreneurial voyage.

SUMMARY:

Cityscape of Triumph is an inspiring entrepreneurial journey that follows Mike, a successful business owner whose world crumbles when his business faces bankruptcy. The narrative unfolds over 27 chapters, each encapsulating a crucial stage in Mike's path to recovery, growth, and triumph.

The story begins with Mike at the pinnacle of success, only to face the harsh reality of business failure. Chapter by chapter, readers witness Mike's initial struggles, emotional turmoil, and reflections on life and goals. The turning point comes when Mike discovers a new passion or opportunity, setting the stage for a dynamic narrative.

As Mike embarks on a new venture, he faces skepticism from friends and family, adding layers of tension to the storyline. Undeterred, he takes the leap into the unknown, leading to initial challenges in the new endeavor. However, Mike's determination grows, propelling the narrative forward.

Chapter by chapter, the story unravels a tapestry of small victories, setbacks, and pivotal moments. Mike forms key alliances and partnerships, begins to see signs of progress, and experiences a major breakthrough for his business. Personal growth and lessons learned become integral to Mike's journey.

The plot takes unexpected turns as obstacles threaten progress, and Mike confronts his fears and doubts. Adapting to changing circumstances, he expands his network and customer base, facing ethical dilemmas and tough decisions along the way. The narrative reaches a climax as Mike gains recognition and respect in the industry.

The story doesn't shy away from new challenges and competition in Chapter 22, creating a riveting narrative. Personal relationships strain under pressure, adding a human touch to the tale. Mike's resilience is tested in Chapter 24, presenting the reader with the raw realities of entrepreneurship.

As the plot unfolds, Mike confronts, adapts, and ultimately overcomes challenges, leading to the expansion of his network and customer base in Chapter 18. Ethical dilemmas become pivotal in Chapter 19, shaping the moral compass of the protagonist.

In Chapter 20, Mike gains recognition and respect in the industry, showcasing the fruits of his perseverance. However, new challenges and competition arise in Chapter 22, adding complexity to the narrative. Personal relationships strain under pressure in Chapter 23, highlighting the emotional toll of entrepreneurship.

The narrative takes a turn in Chapter 24 as Mike's resilience is tested by a series of challenges. He confronts fears, doubts, and adapts to changing circumstances in Chapter 25. The story reaches a climactic point in Chapter 25, where Mike faces the biggest challenge yet, presenting a pivotal moment in his journey.

Triumphantly, Chapter 26 unfolds as Mike resolves conflicts and overcomes obstacles. The narrative crescendos in Chapter 27, where not only does Mike's business survive, but it thrives. Major successes are celebrated, marking the culmination of a journey marked by resilience, innovation, and unwavering determination.

"Resilience in City Lights" is a captivating novel that explores the highs and lows of entrepreneurship, showcasing the human spirit's ability to endure, adapt, and ultimately triumph in the face of adversity.